Women Around the Well

How women's sacred circles are changing the world

by Penelope Genter and Others

Dedicated to all the women in my family circle - grandmother, mother, aunt, sister, daughters, daughters-in-law, step-daughters, and great-granddaughters who carry the light in the world.

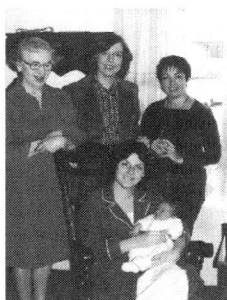

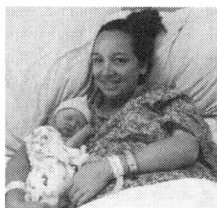

5

JOEF Publications

An Imprint of Journey of Enlightenment Foundation

P. O. Box 21603

Sedona, AZ 86341

Contents

Around the Well 11

I Thirst... 13

The Magic of Women's Sacred Circles 19

MILLIONTH CIRCLE...21

The Community of Women - 31

Congressional Caucus for Women's Issues 33

Sisters of a common need - Albuquerque Soul Sisters 35

Circles around a common belief or theme -Women in the Circle of Mary Magdalene 37

Sedona Sophia Circle...39

Sophia's Sacred Sound Celebration...46

Book Club - Magdalene Mystery School 53

VACATION – RETREAT – REBOOT 57

Passing the baton to the next generation 61

Women Speak 67

Mentoring a New Generation of Women Leaders 69

So where do we go from here?..73

Resources: 75

About the author 77

"The Western Woman will save the world."
The Dalai Lama

One of the ways we are doing this is through the sacred circles of the conscious women of the new paradigm.

Around the Well

Wells are the life of the people where the substance of the Earth Mother pours forth for her daughters. It is in the gathering of this lifeblood of the people that women find nurturing in both physical and spiritual sense. It has ever been so...

Since ancient times women have shared wisdom with sisters around the well, and in the red tent, about their lives, their visions, their challenges and their dreams. The Divine Feminine lives in the circles of the women who hold her veil. It is where we learn the mysteries, the gifts, and the secrets and the power of the Feminine Face of God.

A world that fails to acknowledge and honor the divine mystery of the feminine, is poorer for the source of all blessings springs from the co-creation of the Divine Masculine and Divine Feminine. Without the balance of the feminine heart, the doingness of the patriarchy is a parched land.

Women are expressing a desire to re-experience the ritual and ceremonies that unite and empower them in the safety of the circle of women. The permission to overcome emotional suppression in the drumming, singing, dancing, and chanting somehow triggers a release of anger, grief and mystical joy that transcends the experience.

Affirming and honoring our differences in a collective context allows the richness of the individual experiences and lessons to nourish the whole. As we set aside the judgements of the ego, we are able to embrace the beauty each sister's vision is adding to our life and see the lessons she transcended as potholes avoided in our own.

I Thirst...

It wasn't until my husband passed that I came to realize the profound benefit I would receive from the sisterhood of wise women. Up until then I had a large, close family that was always there to hear, offer council and wisdom in times of uncertainty. My husband was a faithful mirror and teacher of the ways of the world and how I was showing up. When that was gone, I felt bereft and began looking for what was next in my life.

I was fortunate in that I was soon invited by other conscious women to join in a circle of elders who were able to share their experiences, wisdom, support, and encouragement as we explored the changing world together. Perhaps the secret to this experience is that they were conscious women and had worked through many of the ego traps that tend to derail such endeavors in other environments.

In our early days we were taught that other women were the "competition" and as such it was unsafe to confide in and give comfort to the "enemy". In this way we cut ourselves off from one of our greatest treasures – the support, companionship, and wisdom of other women.

In the '50's and '60's it was all about image. We wanted the fairytale – the perfect marriage – the perfect family – the perfect life. Anything that did not reflect that was hidden from view and we fretted or self-medicated in silence. Girlfriends spoke of superficial things that usually skirted real issues and therefore real solutions.

By the '70's and '80's the windows were opening but we were not quite sure how to go about dealing with this new-found freedom. The search for integrity was a massive adjustment as the pendulum swung from one extreme to the other and we tried to find our place in this world that didn't quite match anything we had been prepared for. We grappled with new definitions of what it meant to be feminine and a "feminist" and how that fit in the life we wanted to lead. As Joseph Campbell put it, *"the old concepts, ideals and emotional meanings no longer fit."*

Many of us found ourselves relocated to places without the family counselors and support systems we had known that had been left behind. We were in a land where there were few guidelines as to how we should interact in this world built on Jell-O. If we were fortunate to come from a loving family with good values, encouragement, and support, the adjustment was relatively easy. We made up new rules and followed a preset moral compass. Others who were not so fortunate went down many dark alleys before finding their path into the light. However, we got here, there were many lessons we had all learned on the way.

Now was time to come together with others who had navigated a steep path and to chart together our sacred journey into the new millennium.

©Dawn DelVecchio Empowered Feminine Leadership Retreats

Women's Circles Then and Now

Women's circles in general are <u>going mainstream</u> across the US. As it turns out, we're all just waking up to a practice that's really ancient, albeit one that fell out of favor for centuries in the Western world. "This ritual of women gathering is so universal," points out Sarah Waxman, founder of <u>At The Well</u>—a network that helps women create their own circles for Rosh Chodesh, a traditional Jewish new-moon meet-up.

According to Ann Landaas Smith, founder and director of <u>Circle Connections</u>, humans have basically been gathering in the round since we began walking upright. "Circles with a sacred center are ancient, the oldest form of social interaction," says the mentor and educator, who also works with <u>Millionth Circle</u>—an organization that helps women to start their own groups. "The fire was in the center as the people cooked and ate their food, heard stories, worshiped their gods and goddesses, and passed down the traditions and wisdom that kept them alive and healthy. The red tent [menstrual tradition] and moon lodges grew in popularity as a sacred space for women and girls to affirm their spirituality and sex.

So, what happened between then and now to make women's circles all but disappear from conventional culture? "We weren't allowed to come together because it made people feel uncomfortable, and we were persecuted for it," says Paula Mallis, circle facilitator and owner of <u>WMN Space</u> in Los Angeles. "Those women that have come before us have paved the way, creating space for this pivotal time where we are shifting, changing and transforming. Of course, that didn't completely stop women from getting together on their own terms, from sewing and quilting circles to tea dates and Mary Kay parties. We were still called to gather, but we weren't allowed to dip into an energy that would offend the power of the masculine," says Mallis.

Fast-forward 20 years, and Waxman believes that Sheryl Sandberg's **Lean In** movement paved the way for our generation to discover women's circles in the present day. They basically showed that by gathering together, setting goals, and talking about our challenges, women could make serious strides at work. And now that lunar everything is trending in a big way, we're starting to bring the more esoteric aspect of old-timey women's circles back into the equation, too.

"I believe the feminine rising is an opportunity for tremendous shifts in consciousness and on our planet," says Mallis. "And though we still have work to do, those women that have come before us have paved the way, creating space for this pivotal time where we are shifting, changing and transforming."

How modern women's circles make you happier...and healthier

As most women's circle attendees will tell you, the experience is a lot different from, say, gossiping at a dinner party or talking shop at a networking event. "It's a very different energy." When we're in a setting where we're not going to compete with each other, there's a hormonal response that we're safe. [And that allows us to] look each other in the eye and talk about real shit that's going on in our lives." Part of this is because of the ritualized nature of a women's circle. Even today's facilitators often bring in ceremonial practices that help create a level playing field and encourage everyone to participate in the discussion.

Yet today's facilitators have also found ways to make the ritual uniquely their own. "I take people through a process that includes identifying an issue that is not serving them, and I give them the tools they need to reframe it," Mallis says. "There are many kinds of circles depending on the needs of the members—they can be support circles, healing and wellness circles, spirituality circles, or action circles. Women's circles are encouraged even within some churches."

And the effects have been profound, which is what leads women to come back again and again. Mallis has seen relationships, new jobs, and creative breakthroughs come out of her circles, which have become so popular that she now hosts multiple sessions for each new and full moon. "My intention is that every woman who walks through the doors at WMN Space has an experience that supports her and empowers her to live her life at the fullest and most authentic level," Mallis says. "WMN Circle is designed so that we may find deeper connections within ourselves and fully experience the magic that happens when like-minded women come together."

While most women's circles today are relegated to yoga studios and living rooms, those in the know expect to see them reaching a wider radius of society in the years to come.

For one, we might see women's circles at work become as prevalent as corporate yoga classes, as more workplaces wise up to the perks of a feminine leadership model based on cooperation and equality. Indeed, Mallis has already started fielding requests from LA-based businesses that want her to lead circles at their offices. "It's based off of what they're seeing online," she says. "I'm like, whoa, *this* corporate company wants to experience a shift? It's been really interesting."

Waxman even envisions doctors prescribing women's circles to their patients in the same way that they now do with meditation, specifically when it comes to treating mental health issues. "We know [so] many women are suffering from depression, loneliness, and anxiety, and this is a ritual that is literally designed to combat that," she says, noting that the circle she attends has helped her in her own lifelong battle with depression. (Just look at all the recent research on telomeres for proof of the health-protective power of strong social connections.)

And ultimately, Waxman hopes that women's circles will have an even bigger impact on healing the world at large. "If we can teach women around the world to be in these real types of communities designed for witnessing each other, [we may be able to convince] different groups of women in conflict to come *together* in these circles," she says. "Can we get Israeli and Palestinian women to practice being in a women's circle together? I don't think the world knows what that would look like, but in a dreaming sense that's *really* powerful." Name a happy hour with that kind of impact—kind of makes you want to rethink your weekend plans, doesn't it?

ERIN MAGNER, APRIL 25, 2018
HTTPS://WWW.WELLANDGOOD.COM/GOOD-ADVICE/WOMENS-CIRCLE-HISTORY-ANCIENT/

A WOMEN'S CIRCLE IS AN INTIMATE GATHERING WHERE WE LEARN NEW WAYS OF SPEAKING, LISTENING + RELATING TO OTHERS.

ONCE FORMED, THE CIRCLE BECOMES A CONTAINER FOR TRUTH TELLING AND SACRED WITNESSING, HEALING AND TRANSFORMATION.

"The Circle is everyday ceremony: the invention of our most ancient Godmothers, who upon witnessing the myriad ways nature exalted this humble shape, claimed it as the spiritual center of their communities. Held by the simple rituals of opening & completion, honoring & appreciation, the Circle acts as a vehicle for both storytelling & transcending our stories. In Circle, we are conversing with the divine."

Baraka Elihu.

The Magic of Women's Sacred Circles

Support, Understanding, Growth, and Inspiration

Our sisters act as "resonators" as described by Sherry Ruth Anderson and Patricia Hopkins in their book, **The Feminine Face of God**. "*A friend or sister or companion so true to her own inner reality, that she inspires them to be faithful to theirs... Many women are coming forward to lead the way. You will be teachers for each other. You will come together in circles to speak your truth to each other. The time has come for women to accept their spiritual responsibility for this planet.*

A circle of women can provide a container for emergence in a way that a woman alone or even a one-to-one relationship cannot. Intimate relationships and even friendships can break, or at least be greatly strained by life changes. But from the combined wisdom and energy of a small group of women who are committed to "hearing each other into speech," continuity and trust can develop that can be relied on over the long term. And witnessing each person's direct knowing of her truth, we can be empowered to live our own."

We are all works in progress – each with our own challenges and baggage. As blind men exploring an elephant, it is by sharing the unique vision of each of the sisters that the greater picture can be observed as well as the hidden path to enlightenment.

What is said in the circle, stays in the circle. Confidentiality allows women to speak their truth, in safety, knowing they will not be criticized or shunned for their beliefs or gossiped about. Confidentially allows women to take verbal risks, explore options, get feedback, and change their minds.

The sacred circle is not a gripe session – quite the opposite! **It about hearing each other** - our doubts, frustrations, challenges and failings as long **as we own our participation in these without blaming others**. This allows the expanded vision of the sisterhood to help us see the lessons and path to growth it is affording us without judgement. By being truly heard, witnessed, and forgiven, we gain the tools we need for growth.

The circle is a practice in discernment, not judgement. Judgement cuts off the free-flow of loving energy. Discernment is the ability to speak, sort, and speak without having to be right or in total agreement. Someone else's views do not have to be right or wrong - they can just be different. It is in our differences we learn empathy, appreciation for each, and expand our world.

Each person takes responsibility for asking the circle for the support she wants or needs and for their perspective on situations she is facing. Perhaps it gives her the courage to finally speak her truth out loud without being shamed or threatened. She becomes the voice for the unheard that resonates through the sisterhood. As these muscles are strengthened, the new speakers of the feminine voice of God are stepping forth into their ascendancy.

Listening without interrupting is a gift we give each other. **Practice listening with your heart to what she is really sharing and not what you can add to the discussion.** The speaker may hold a talking object as the others listen until this becomes automatic for the group.

Sisters are there not to criticize, but to facilitate each other's growth and understanding, to lovingly offer suggestions, to help them see the deeper issue that is being experienced, and applaud the positive choices made in their lives. There is no room for negativity, criticism, or competition.

As **we celebrate our differences** we tap in to the common bonds of womanhood. We foster development of our individual gifts and create an atmosphere of discovery and growth. Sisters are encouraged to step back and view situations from a higher place, without judgement, fear, and projection in order to see through to the lesson in love this is showing us.

Our bodies are channels to receive and give out divine energy. As we pray, sing, and dance together, we embody this divine energy and cast it wide for the upliftment of the greater community. This is the new paradigm of sacred women's circles.

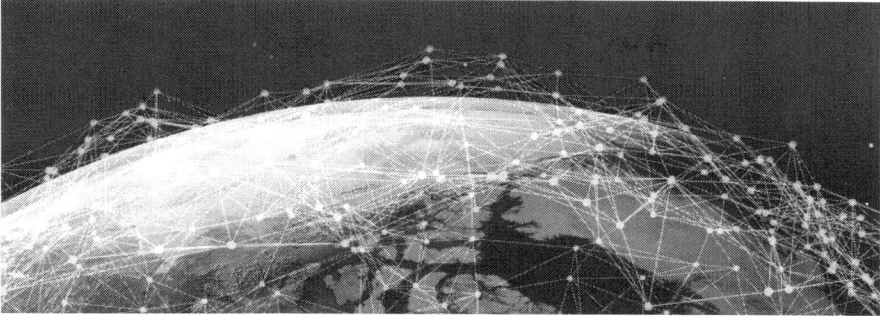

MILLIONTH CIRCLE

The Millionth Circle is a grass-roots, international volunteer organization of women who believe that circles are the means through which world consciousness will change.

The millionth circle refers to the circle whose (metaphoric) formation tips the scales and shifts planetary consciousness. The phrase comes from Jean Shinoda Bolen's book 'The Millionth Circle: How to Change Ourselves and The World'. The Millionth Circle is a group of women who, since 2001, have volunteered their time to hold this vision through their participation in monthly virtual circles and annual in-person circles where a deepening of the circle experience occurs. By holding this Mother Circle they anchor the concept of a million circles.

OUR INTENTIONS

Circles encourage connection and cooperation among their members through dialogue and deep listening. Circles cultivate an environment of equality where compassionate solutions to individual, community, and world problems can be explored.

We believe that circles support each member to find their own voice and to live more courageously.

We intend:

- to seed and nurture circles, wherever possible, in order to cultivate equality, sustainable livelihoods, preservation of the earth and peace for all.
- to bring the circle process into United Nations accredited non-governmental organizations and a 5th UN World Conference on Women.
- to connect circles so they may know themselves as a part of a larger movement to shift consciousness in the world.

OUR VISION

A proliferation of circles with a spiritual center becomes a worldwide healing force by bringing feminine values of relationship, nurturing, equality, cooperation, and interdependency into the global culture.

Circles create what Margaret Wheatley calls, 'islands of sanity' in which people feel supported to care for themselves, their families, their communities and their planet.

Feeling this support they are empowered to be leaders for positive change. Our aim is to help seed and nurture a tipping point of circles everywhere.

CIRCLE GUIDELINES

To participate in a circle, all you need is the desire, the willingness to attend the gatherings and to agree to follow circle principles. Each group determines their own guidelines. Following are some agreements that have helped circles to function more successfully for all participants.

- Create a circle.
- Consider it a sacred space.
- One person speaks at a time.

- Speak and listen from the heart.
- Encourage and welcome diverse points of view.
- Listen with discernment instead of judgment.
- When in doubt or need, pause and silently ask for guidance.
- Share leadership and resources.
- Decide together how decisions will be made.
- Work toward consensus when possible.
- Offer experience instead of advice.
- Decide together what is to be held in confidence.
- Speak from your own experience and beliefs rather than speaking for others.
- Open and close the circle by hearing each voice. (Check-ins and check-outs.)

CIRCLE PRINCIPLES

The following are some suggestions for creating a successful circle:

- Create sacred space. This includes physically preparing a space to accommodate the participants in a circle, usually with a centerpiece or altar.
- Listen with compassion and for wisdom. This includes listening without an agenda, suspending judgment, being curious and finding the underlying meaning in others' statements. Also, it is listening for wisdom as it comes through each participant.
- Speak from your heart and experience. Speak one at a time. This includes saying what is true for you and speaking to the center of the circle, not to another individual. We offer our experience and feelings to the circle, not our advice. Also, we speak one at a time and invoke a talking piece when needed, to ensure that all are heard.

- Invite silence and reflection when needed, in you and in the circle. This includes listening to our own inner guidance before speaking. Also, we request silence and reflection in the circle when we feel it is needed.

- Take responsibility for your experience and your impact on the circle. This includes demonstrating self-respect and self-restraint. We self-monitor to ensure that our needs and expectations are being met. We ensure our contribution adds to the positive experience of all in the circle.

- Keep the confidence of the circle. This refers to our confidentiality agreements. What is spoken in the circle, stays in the circle to help ensure a safe environment for sharing our experiences and feelings.

- Make decisions, when needed, by consensus. This refers to our decision-making process. Should a circle need to make a decision, it is generally desirable to come to a consensus. These guidelines can be used as a starting point for group agreements in any circle, knowing that each group will add or delete as they see fit.

- Each circle contributes to the Millionth Circle, the tipping point, and the morphic field that makes it easier and easier for others to start one. Millions of circles with a sacred center have been created around the world. They are ancient, found in every indigenous culture and in the women's spirituality movement. They are found in innovative organizations. There is a global women's movement that is a mighty force for positive change and you can be a part by simply saying yes. Starting a circle is easy and will be successful when you use Circle Principles and Guidelines. If you have questions or want professional help contact us. We look forward to you being part of the Millionth Circle.

  -
- For more information:
  Lauren Oliver
  Ashland, Oregon
  lauren@circleworks.net

Ann Smith
Naples, Florida
annlsmith714@gmail.com
- JOIN US on Facebook
- https://www.facebook.com/MillionthCircle/

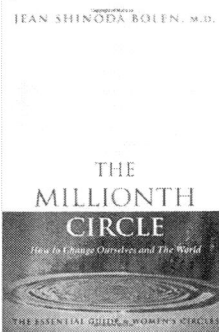

The Millionth Circle: How to Change Ourselves and The World--The Essential Guide to Women's Circles

"The Millionth Circle," writes Bolen, "depends upon a simple hypothesis: when a critical number of people change how they think and behave, the culture will also, and a new era begins. Once the principles are understood, the significance of women's circles can be appreciated as a revolutionary-evolutionary movement that is hidden in plain sight."
Royalties from sales of The Millionth Circle donated to The Millionth Circle Initiative.

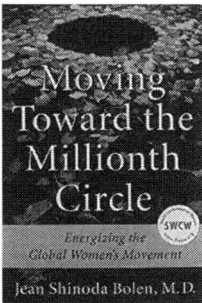

Moving Toward the Millionth Circle: Energizing the Global Women's Movement

Moving Toward the Millionth Circle inspires and enlists women to be millionth circle, heart-centered activists in order to energize a 5th World Conference on Women in the 21st Century. The conference is not a goal in and of itself, but a means toward valuing the feminine to bring about a tipping point. There is more of a focus on activism and how these circles can help to sustain and support (and be a sanctuary for) women working for change in their lives and in the world.

The circles of women around us weave invisible nets of love that carry us when we're weak and sing with us when we are strong.

~Sark

Breathe it in

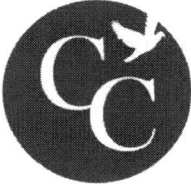

Circle Connections
Circles Connecting for Peace and Justice

The 'New Story' is brought to life by the Circle Model

The 'New Story' is a more collaborative model that has room for an emergent design. It is an egalitarian way of being with one another where everyone works together and is honored for their gifts. The power, the resources, the decision-making, and the work all are shared. This ensures full participation, personal growth and unlimited creativity.

In Circle...

- There is no top and no bottom, just one fluid dynamic system
- The network is formed around a common passion
- Leaders emerge naturally and only inspire to direct and make the group cohesive. They act as a guiding part of a greater whole, not as a director over.
- Groups are more fluid and act from a common commitment to Circle Principles
- Self-sustaining
- Reorganizations happen organically all the time and are easy.
- Conflict resolution and Win/Win Communication is innate in the structure

Through Circle...

- **We become better communicators**
- **Build healthier relationships, deepen trust, and appreciate differences**
- **Become more compassionate decision makers and problem solvers**
- **Develop more balanced, meaningful, and passionate lives**
- **Contribute to our communities**
- **Expand our authenticity, build confidence and a empower healthy self esteem**

The Anchoress Circle in Chartres, France

Circles provide the common ground for all to be truly heard and offers a respectful way of coming together to find new solutions to problems, co-create new resources, events and programs, and close the gap between opposing sides. The **Circle Process** shifts the focus from the 'Old Story' of 'forcing' and **'power-over'** to the 'New Story' of 'allowing' and **'power-with'**.

It seems that the challenges we face today are calling for a shift to a more gentle and conscious way of being with one another if we are to connect and create a new earth.

- Now is the time for women to **collaborate and co-create**, daring to bring forward and give voice to our most authentic and creative self.
- Circle Connections provides an active evolutionary community, a modern day Well, in which women (and the men who love them) can connect, up-lift, and support women
on this journey.
- We inform, inspire, and encourage women to connect and embrace their innate power to lead in all facets of their life, leaning on the Power of Circle in their own spiritual development within their family and intimate relationships within their personal and professional community, locally and globally.
- At Circle Connections we honor that each woman has an individual calling that shapes the form of her leadership and fully support her in putting her passion into action.
- We are committed to bringing forward Circles as mainstream and promote compassionate connections as the means through which we will mutually and collaboratively create a new earth, one circle, one connection, one step at a time.

http://circleconnections.com/circles/why-circles/

The Community of Women -

As Sherry Ruth Anderson and Patricia Hopkins wrote in **The Feminine Face of God**, "*It is from those who walk beside us that we can gain the strength and courage to remain true to our purpose. And what many women today are discovering as they "dig a new-way path" it is not a teacher, or guru, or guide, but a "resonator", a friend or sister or companion so true to her own inner reality that she inspires them to be faithful to theirs. Somehow the resonator calls us to our true selves, reminding us and reflecting to us our deepest possibilities, asking the difficult questions and encouraging us to take action.*"

In the presence of a person that is REAL, you take off your veils of illusion... It is soul meeting soul.

Dorothy Maclean, co-founder of the Findhorn Foundation in Scotland that I met there in 1997 said "*Communities in the past were generally founded by one magnetic or very wise person, and the people would sit at the feet of such person and do what they said. But I see a new type of community emerging, one in which we each tune in to our own higher self and no one is higher or better than anyone else, a leaderless community where all are leaders... I don't think you can be a properly functioning member of a group unless you've found your own individuality. Otherwise you're a weak link, you're leaning on the group because you haven't found your own center.*"

To have community, there must be a commitment to work through disagreements and to care about each other. Truth comes through our sharing stories, music, thoughts, and the relationships among us. As we heal our separation, we heal ourselves and bring peace to the world.

Congressional Caucus for Women's Issues

The **Congressional Caucus for Women's Issues** is a bipartisan membership organization within the House of Representatives committed to advancing women's interests in Congress.

Electoral participation data indicates that for more than 50 years, women have been voting in larger numbers than men. The CCWI was intended to address descriptive representation. With such few women in Congress, the legislative agenda was not representative of the wants and needs of female constituents. It was also a concern that the female representatives faced issues that wouldn't be addressed by the party organizations already established within Congress.

The Congressional Women's Caucus is an important, bipartisan forum to discuss major policy issues of our day with a focus on how these issues impact women and families, In the past, this caucus has been a driving force for a strong Violence Against Women Act and for the Children's Health Insurance Program. Today, women in America still face serious obstacles in the workplace and academia, In the House, they are working to address this by expanding opportunities, increasing flexibility, removing barriers, and empowering the next generation.

Working together to support the needs of women and families is a cornerstone of our country's overall success collaborating in creating legislation that supports the goals of this Caucus including supporting fairness and equality for women."

Founded in 1977, the Congressional Caucus for Women's Issues has been a leading advocate on issues advancing the lives of women and families. Caucus members have helped pass legislation securing tougher child support enforcement, promoting women's health, helping women business owners, and protecting victims of domestic violence and sexual assault. The caucus works closely with the Women's Policy Inc., a nonprofit, nonpartisan public policy organization whose mission is to bring women policymakers together across party lines to work on issues of importance to women and their families.

Goals when created

- remain bipartisan in order to be taken seriously by party leadership, women's special interest organizations, and the media
- include many congresswomen to bring a diversity of ideas and connections
- encourage negotiation and accommodation of diverse ideas
- support among women legislators for policies about women's issues
- physical space where congresswomen could interact
- increase visibility of caucus through contact with White House, administration, and congressional leaders

Sisters of a common need - Albuquerque Soul Sisters

When times seem uncertain, we always reconnect to our sense of inner-knowing which is where we store our truth. With sisters who affirm and support your growth and understanding and share a vision, you have an opportunity to magnify this ability and to make giant leaps in your spiritual life.

After my husband died, I reached out to others who I knew to be conscious. It was agreed that **each was to invite two women who we believed to share a great integrity and vision of truth**. They in turn could invite two each until we had twelve women. Though we did not know each other well, we would soon share a great adventure. The only commitment was that we would show up in truth and love for each other.

We created a safe space where we came to know, appreciate, and celebrate our differences, for they gave us an opportunity to see life beyond our experience. Some of the women had psychic abilities that allowed them to see and describe to the others their visions as we journeyed together. By sharing our knowledge on an unfamiliar subject, we all became privy to the experience through the eyes of our sisters and learned and grew together. It became an atmosphere of discovery and growth as we leap-frogged each other on the spiritual path.

Together we ventured into connected areas in the community and did ceremonies on the land as well as visited sacred sites. This was a soul group that had come back together as planned to learn and grow together.

Circles around a common belief or theme -Women in the Circle of Mary Magdalene

In 2011 I went on a pilgrimage to southern France "in the footsteps of Mary Magdalene". Upon returning, I did a presentation at Unity of Sedona. Over 60 people showed up, many of them curious and wanting to know more about Mary Magdalene, who she really was, and why they were so attracted to and intrigued by her story.

Using the book *14 Steps to Awaken the Sacred Feminine – Women in the Circle of Mary Magdalene* by Joan Norton and Margaret Starbird as a guide, we began a monthly meeting at Unity, exploring the mysteries of the Magdalene.

We came to understand that many of us were part of a soul group that had spent a previous lifetime with Jesus and Mary Magdalene and had come back together in service to the divine. Several had been drawn to the Languedoc in France. One conducted tours there. We began a shared library of books on the subject so that we could share the things we discovered.

We became a sisterhood of shared insights and experiences that was awakening deeper truths in each other.

The monthly circle replaced a previous women's group that had outgrown the old paradigm of tired studies and arts and crafts. The new group continued for five years into it too morphed into something different.

Sedona Sophia Circle

Several leaders from the previous Magdalene Circle recognized a need to open to the greater community of women. We created a sisterhood of conscious wisdom keepers of Sedona of every faith, open to all in the community who carried that light. It was creating a new paradigm for women to support, learn, and grow with others of similar intent in loving and respectful ways. Not a "gripe session", but a safe way for sisters to come together in service to each other in our growth and understanding. **It was not meant for commercial, political, or self-promotional purposes, but a weaving together of the divine aspects of the feminine in cooperation rather than competition. We were creating a new template for women's circles.**

As to how we structured this...

The founding sisters set the purpose and the structure of the group, secured the facility for weekly meetings and were responsible for advertising it to the community, logistics of meetings, and supervising the programs. One sister acted as a "cat herder" who directed the activities and kept everything moving and on time. With chairs in a circle, in turn each sister was passed a rose quartz heart which meant that she had the floor for **five minutes** to check in with whatever she needed to share. The rest of us LISTENED and did not respond until she had shared from her heart, and then ONLY if we could offer something meaningful and relevant – not just to make conversation. Meetings were structured so that all of the sisters were heard, honored, and appreciated for their unique gifts and abilities in a loving environment.

The third Monday of each month was a community **Soul Weaving**. Light workers from all areas of the community were invited to join us for soup, salad, and sharing. It was getting to know each other so that we could come together more deeply and build a network of caring, referral, and support for sisters on the path. We checked in with our visions, joys, struggles, challenges, where we need help, and where we could help, and what we were doing in the community and our lives.

Sedona is blessed to have many masters who travel the world sharing their sacred gifts. Every other month there was a sister from the community who gifted the sisters with her knowledge and abilities. She was allowed to have flyers for her commercial services, but it was about sharing the work of the goddess in the world.

Suggested schedule for the **Soul Weaving** evenings :
6:00-6:15 Check in
6:15-6:30 Attunement ceremony and announcements
6:30-7:00 Dinner
7:00-8:00 Soul weaving in small groups of max. 11-12 women. Each sister has 5 min to check in.
8:00-8:30 Community weaving and Circle of Consciousness
8:30-9:00 Networking and Cleanup

Suggested donation for **Soul Weaving** evening was $5 to cover expenses. Any overage went to a designated community charity.

Soul Weaving sharing

Community Salad bowl and homemade vegetarian soup

Invoking the Sacred

Ceremony

Healing

Life Dramas

Sophia's Sacred Sound Celebration

Sophia's Sacred Sound
Celebration for Women

*Sharing SOUNDWAVES to transform
ourselves and our community through*

DRUMMING • TONING
DANCING • SINGING
SACRED CEREMONY

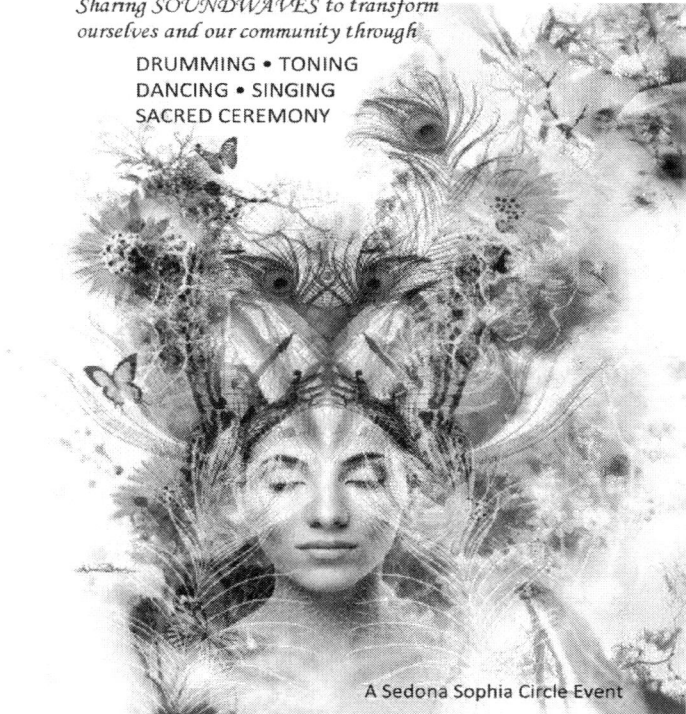

A Sedona Sophia Circle Event

Monday, March 7th ~ Doors open at 5:45pm
360 Brewer Rd / Keep Sedona Beautiful building
Suggested Energy Exchange $5 ♥ Gifting Sedona Area Homeless Alliance

Drumming Circles

Every other month we invited the men to join us

Fire Ceremony

Make a Joyful Noise

Book Club - Magdalene Mystery School

One of the time-proven ways women (and a few men) have gathered together over time has been to review and discuss books of a common interest. Several of our Magdalene sisters decided to take this to a greater depth by studying together some of the more significant books that had the greatest vibrational frequency around the Magdalene Mysteries and discuss our revelations in our own pursuit of truth. The sisters we invited we know to be serious students of the mysteries. Some have written books, led seminars, traveled and led tours to the Magdalene sites and are well-versed in the subject.

Since we knew that this would go beyond the casual inquiry of a normal book club, we agreed upon certain criteria: We would meet once a month on the second Tuesday. Everyone would attend at least every other month in order to keep continuity. We would record the meetings on Zoom so that those away could either tune in on-line or catch up with the recorded version when convenient.

All sisters agreed to read the assigned material and come ready to discuss it and the implications. We began with ***Anna, Voice of the Magdalenes*** and ***Anna, Grandmother of Jesus*** by Clair Heartsong and Catherine Ann Clement. We then read ***Jesus, the Book***, then ***Jesus the Forgotten Years*** by Durga Holzhauser and Frank Eickermann. All calibrated very high on the energetic scale.

Several of the sisters are channels and brought in information that was helpful to the group. Several sisters are proficient dowsers and helped us calibrate the energetic vibration of truth on a numeric scale to help in discerning between various opposing opinions. Together we came to consensus of what we believed to be truth that allowed us to put these pebbles in the mosaic.

We embraced and welcomed several touring soul sisters who showed up in Sedona for events they were giving and shared the wisdom of Sophia with her sisters. We created a chalice of feminine wisdom and loving awareness through our ceremonies, anointings, and sacred practices that have forever united the feminine.

As we continued into our second year together, we realized that we had become a family of soul sisters. We see, recognize, and applauded the growth in each other as we continued to blossom into a clearer reflection of our divine selves. We recognized the nurturing experience of breaking bread together and decided to bring salads to share around the family table as we catch up on the events in each of our lives. We always allow time for each sister to check in and reveal the challenges and the miracles that are taking place around and through us.

The diversity of the group has been one of our greatest blessings as we bring spiritual experiences from every faith and journey. Several women self-selected out of the group because they realized they were not yet up to the experience. Though sisters have moved in and out of the circle as lives and soul journeys progress, we remain divinely guided and a constant and touch-stone for all and the place where truth and love are practiced.

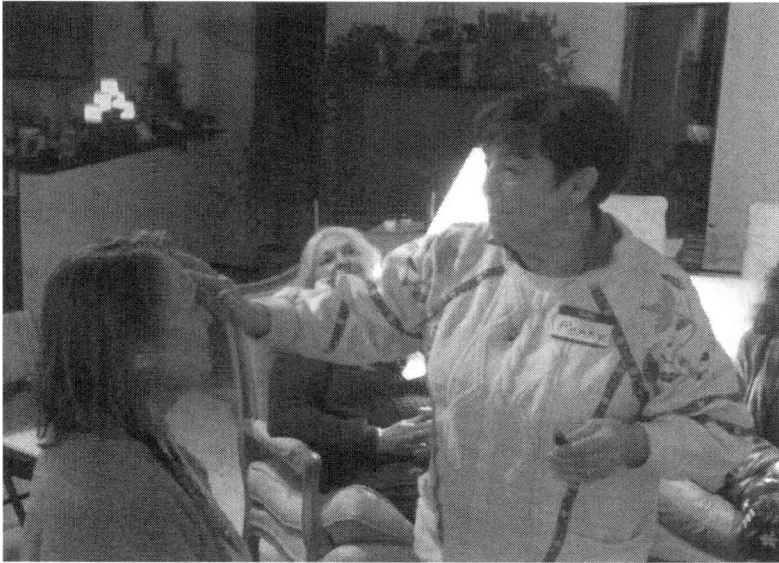

VACATION – RETREAT – REBOOT

WHAT BETTER PLACE THAN AN EXOTIC LOCALE WITH OTHER LIKE-MINDED WOMEN FROM AROUND THE WORLD WHO COME TOGETHER TO CHANGE THEIR WORLD AND THEREFORE THE GREATER WORLD...

Dawn DelVecchio facilitates Priestess Training Retreats in Thailand, Sedona, and Bali.

"The Divine Feminine is Re-Awakening here on Mother Earth and Empowered Feminine Leaders are Needed Urgently" ~ Dawn DelVecchio

A RETREAT LIKE THIS IS FOR YOU IF ...

- *You've been on a deep, spiritual, soul-searching journey, (maybe for more lives than this one).*
- *You probably know a lot about many things.*
- *You're ready to go to the next level ... a deeper level.*
- *You know you are meant for a more meaningful, impactful kind of leadership.*
- *You are feeling called to step up and serve.*

- Now it's time to truly deepen into your Soul's Wisdom and Truth. It is time to learn more, get connected, to integrate and be able to move in your life (and your life's work) as an Empowered, Feminine Leader.

THIS IS AN OPPORTUNITY FOR WOMEN TO ...

- Deepen your connection to the Sacred Feminine within you.
- Strengthen bonds of Sisterhood.
- Learn Chants & Processes in order to Create Magical, Transformative Experiences for Yourself and for Others.
- Learn Effective Techniques for Healing and Awakening your Personal Power.
- Gain a Deeper Understanding of your Self – and your Emerging Gifts as a Leader.
- Explore a Variety of Tools for Insight and Understanding.
- Cultivate a Strong Connection to Earth.
- Strengthen your Self Trust and Belly Wisdom.
- Create a Container which Allows you to Integrate All of your Knowing in Service to a Higher Calling.

You will walk away from our week together feeling confident that you can take these skills and tools back to your community in order to facilitate Healing and Transformation as a Priestess – an Empowered Feminine Leader.

"WHAT IS A PRIESTESS?"
by Dawn DelVecchio

To me, the word "Priestess" is associated with a woman who serves her community in a spiritual capacity.

She is a female leader who honors the Sacred Feminine aspect of Divinity. She may or may not have been "initiated" into a particular lineage, but she has studied long, works on herself personally and has skills and experience in various healing modalities, counselling, ceremonial facilitation, and at least a pinch of magic.

Her service may be her primary vocation, or her avocation.

A Priestess can hold space for others as they move through the more painful emotions and difficult life experiences we all face from time to time.

A Priestess owns her own shit. She does not play the "blame game" or devote time and energy to judging others for their human foibles.

She has faced her own shadow with courage. She has fallen down in life and picked herself back up more than once. She has overcome difficult, often painful losses, and she has mastered her skills and abilities through dedication, consistency and time.

A Priestess takes good care of herself and her family. She enjoys the pleasures of life and does not take vows of poverty or chastity, for she understands that All Acts of Love and Beauty are Sacred.

WHAT A PRIESTESS IS NOT...

A Priestess is not a woman who merely dresses the part because it's intriguing or fun.

Being a Priestess is not a fashion statement or a trendy lifestyle choice. Priestesses are not "clicky," nor do they put forth their work in order to achieve ego-gratifying renown.

While abundance is the blessing bestowed upon the Priestess (including financial abundance) for doing her Soul's Sacred Work, the true path of a Priestess is not for those seeking rock-star fame or fortune with a Priestess "brand."

In times such as these, the true Path of a Priestess is not for the faint of heart.

Being a Priestess is a spiritual dedication. It is a commitment that may at times call you to draw up courage and strength from depths you didn't even know you had.

As with all Spiritual Callings, one is Called to the role of Priestess. It is a dedication to Spiritual Service.

Dawn DelVecchio, Author, Teacher, Priestess.
http://PriestessSchool.info/Thailand19
http://DawnDelVecchio.com

Passing the baton to the next generation

WOMEN'S CIRCLES ARE THE NEW GIRLS' NIGHT OUT—HERE'S
HOW TO HOST ONE AT HOME

When it comes to hanging with your girlfriends, cocktails and gossip are starting to seem as antiquated as a pre-cell phone era *Sex and the City* episode.

Instead, we're going on workout dates, meditating en masse, and, even more recently, joining women's circles—all-female gatherings that often involve rituals, intention setting, learning, and sharing (with no judginess allowed).

A growing number of women are choosing to throw them in their own homes.

Shel Pink, founder of "slow beauty" brand SpaRitual, is one of them. "I was seeking a spiritual connection with friends—an expansive, creative, and open-minded experience grounded in tradition," says Pink, when asked why she started hosting monthly circles in her Hollywood Hills home last year.

She adds that going deep with your girlfriends is truly vital in the age of overstuffed schedules and surface-level social media friendships. "I'm interested in knowing *people*, not their curated online personas. Each time we meet as a group, we give ourselves an opportunity to slow down."

And those three hours of bonding time aren't just fun—they might also make you a better human. "Spending time with people you enjoy, with whom you can be open and supportive, is a profound [aspect] of self-care," says Pink. "And when we care for ourselves in deep, meaningful ways, we are best able to care for others and the world."

1. Plan it by the stars

Pink's crew gathers on the new moon each month to honor the Jewish holiday Rosh Chodesh—but even if you're not religious, she says the new moon is traditionally an auspicious time to circle up. "It is a celebration of renewal for women, by women; a sacred time to reflect and set intentions for the month ahead," she says.

2. Keep your invite list tight

Pink finds that 15 women is the winning number for her circles, and she stresses it's important to keep the invite list the same each time. "A deep trust develops over time when a consistent group of women gets together regularly and have shared experiences," she says. And when you trust the ones you're with, you're bound to open up more—and create more profound connections.

3. Pick a theme

To help set the tone of your gathering, it helps to choose a theme that can run throughout the evening—anything from joy to forgiveness to gratitude could work. In Pink's case, "We begin by discussing the theme, and then come together with a candle-lighting ceremony that opens with a blessing. We go around the circle and light each other's candles, and whoever would like to add to the blessing is welcome to do so. This ceremony is beautiful and is a way to pause, reflect, and set personal intentions for the month ahead."

4. Bring in a special guest

Pink recommends hiring a healer, speaker, or expert to lead a mini-workshop relating to the theme—think sound baths, guided meditations, or poetry classes. (Most teachers are open to hosting small group sessions). "I personally select each guest speaker based on the theme to help us to deepen our connection to it," she says. And don't be shy about reaching out to your social media wellness crush—they'll probably be stoked to join you. "A few of the speakers have become personal friends of mine," adds Pink.

5. Don't forget the food

Whether it's catered, potluck, or prepared by the hostess, eating together is a big part of the women's circle experience. A little healthy indulgence is welcome— even encouraged. "Wine is *always* served," says Pink. We'll toast to that!

https://www.wellandgood.com/good-advice/womens-circles-hosting-how-to/

alamy stock photo

Lean In Circles

Lean In Circles are **small groups of women who meet regularly to learn and grow together**. They are focused on utilizing the power of peer support, mentoring and shared experiences. Women in over 160 countries have joined the Lean In community. Members meet in small groups called Lean In Circles about once a month to support each other and learn new skills. They talk openly about their ambitions and encourage each other to take on new challenges. Together, they are going further and standing up for equality.

Circles are a place where women can be unapologetically ambitious. Where we can give voice to our dreams and find the encouragement to start chasing them. They're a place for sharing ideas, gaining skills, seeking advice, and showing solidarity. Most of all, they're a place where we help each other become our very best selves. Whatever your goal—whether you're working toward a promotion or building your confidence, reentering the workforce or starting a business—your Circle will help you get there.

Members meet once a month in small groups to support each other and learn new skills. Circles are everywhere. We're a community of women who meet in nearly every country and at some of the largest companies. Circles can meet over coffee at your home, in a lunch series at work, or in virtual meet-up with people who share similar interests. And we know they work: 85% of members say their Circle has made a positive impact on their life.

Circles are as unique as the women who start them. But they're all about accomplishing more—together. Freelancers in France are sharing tips, introducing each other to clients, and practicing negotiations. Latinas in Silicone Valley with decades of experience are mentoring the next generation. Students in India are taking on gender stereotypes and going further—faster. Women and men are meeting in P&G offices from Cincinnati to Singapore to advance women leaders and combat gender bias. Circle members around the world stand shoulder to shoulder to advance equality.

Women in Circles are...

- more confident and ambitious
- more likely to ask for—and receive—promotions
- more aware of the role that gender plays at work
- According to Women in the Workplace 2017, co-authored by LeanIn.Org and McKinsey & Company. https://leanin.org/circles
-

Women Speak

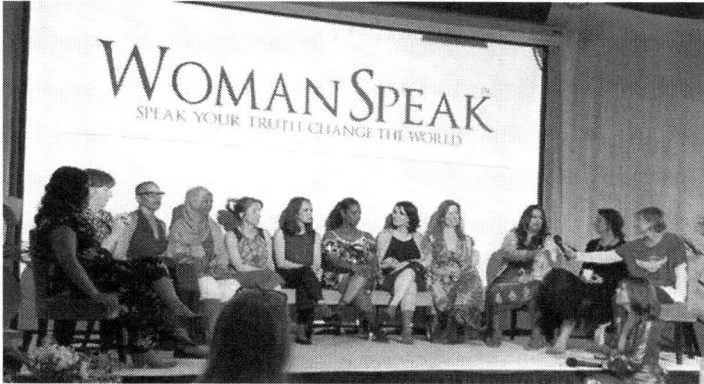

- For too long, public speaking trainings have fostered a masculine model of what leadership and professionalism looks and feels like. This can have a detrimental effect on the self-esteem of women and girls who desire to speak up and lead.

- This sparks feeling of self-doubt, a lack of valuing the wisdom within, and a resistance to speaking up. It erodes a woman's sense of inner freedom to lead and share her mind publicly

- They provide an alternative for women to harness the power of their feminine energy, rather than hide or deny it, as they speak up to lead and effect change.

- The founder KC Baker has taught and spoken about this unique body of work at the United Nations, Women@Microsoft, TEDxWomen, and more.

- Women around the world are wanting support in speaking up and leading as who they truly are, rather than feeling like they have to suppress a part of themselves in order to fit into a masculine model of leadership.

Training
The curriculum supports women in clarifying and owning the value of their ideas. They teach women how to prepare and deliver talks, presentations and communications that move, impact and influence their listeners.

Support
They support women in feeling confident and free to speak up & be themselves in a variety of settings: public talks on stages, panel discussions, group/team meetings, fundraising conversations and more.

Challenges
They help women to transform fear, doubt and resistance to sharing their voices into natural confidence and charisma. We deal with the unique challenges that come up for women around sharing their voices in the presence of men.

Celebration
They do so in a very supportive, celebratory and fun environment!

http://womanspeak.com/

Mentoring a New Generation of Women Leaders

The Girl Scout Difference

Girl Scouts offers the best leadership development experience for girls in the world.

Girl Scouts unleashes the G.I.R.L. (Go-getter, Innovator, Risk-taker, Leader)™ in every girl, preparing her for a lifetime of leadership—from taking a night-time hike under the stars to accepting a mission on the International Space Station; from lobbying the city council with her troop to holding a seat in Congress; from running her own cookie business today to tackling cybersecurity tomorrow.

Our Girl Scout Leadership Experience is a one-of-a-kind leadership development program for girls, with proven results. It is based on time-tested methods and research-backed programming that help girls take the lead—in their own lives and in the world.

Research shows that girls learn best in an all-girl, girl-led, and girl-friendly environment. Girl Scouts is a place where she'll practice different skills, explore her potential, take on leadership positions—and even feel allowed to fail, dust herself off, get up, and try again.

Girl Scouts is proven to help girls thrive in five key ways as they:
 Develop a strong sense of self.

Seek challenges and learn from setbacks.

Display positive values.

Form and maintain healthy relationships.

Identify and solve problems in the community.

The inclusive, all-female environment of a Girl Scout troop creates a safe space where girls can try new things, develop a range of skills, take on leadership roles, and just be themselves.

Girl Scouts takes the potential of girls, combines it with robust skill-building programming, and adds caring adult mentors and strong female role models.

Everything a Girl Scout does centers around STEM, the outdoors, development of life skills, and entrepreneurship, and is designed to meet her where she is now and to grow along with her.

Whether she's building a robotic arm, coding her first app, building a shelter in the backcountry, or packing for her first hike, a Girl Scout has an exciting array of choices to suit her interests at every age.

At Girl Scouts, "Can I?" quickly turns into "I will!" as girls transform their ideas into action, turn their questions into adventure, and grow their confidence through practice. And with more than 50 million other G.I.R.L.s to cheer them on every step of the way, there's no limit to what she can accomplish.

Girl Scouts works. It's the best leadership experience for girls in the world for one very good reason: because it's girl-led!

Unleash her inner leader.

As a volunteer, you'll introduce girls to new experiences and help them unleash their inner G>I>R>L> (Go-getter, Innovator, Risk-taker, Leader)™ to take the lead and change the world.

You'll be their cheerleader, guide, and mentor, helping them develop crucial skills and confidence to launch them into a lifetime of leadership. Imagine the excitement, the memories made, and the *impact*—this is what you'll share as a Girl Scout volunteer.

www.girlscouts.org/

Personally, I know of few things that allowed me to experience the growth of myself and my daughters as the years I/we spent in Girl Scouts, as a Brownie, Girl Scout, Girl Scout Leader, and Camp Director. It is where we step out of our mundane lives and are allowed to learn and grow in the company of other women and women-in-training as to what it means to be a woman of abilities, honor, and service to our community. I am forever grateful.

So where do we go from here?

Not in many generations have women been so motivated to change their world for the better. One of the feminine attributes is our ability to step back and see the inconsistencies in life and imagine the possibilities of the future. Certainly, the political and social outrages that are coming to the surface and finally being addressed on the world stage are an impetus for women to get involved in their world beyond their front door.

Many are unsure about how to take the first steps. I might suggest that they begin by "circling the wagons" with sisters who they know and trust. What do they and others see as needs and challenges not being addressed responsibly in their sphere of influence? What might be done to address the situation differently? Who has pieces and insights that might change the direction and face of that reality? Who is willing to step forward? Who can help?

Even if your knees shake...

"Never doubt that a small group of thoughtful, committed citizens can change the world; indeed, it's the only thing that ever has."   Margaret Mead

"Let us remember: One book, one pen, one child, and one teacher can change the world." Malala Yousafzai

"Every great dream begins with a dreamer. Always remember, you have within you the strength, the patience, and the passion to reach for the stars to change the world."   Harriet Tubman

"Change will not come if we wait for some other person or some other time. We are the ones we've been waiting for. We are the change that we seek."

Barack Obama

"You must be the change you wish to see in the world."

Mahatma Gandhi

Resources:

https://leanin.org/circles

DawnDelVecchio@gmail.com

http://priestessschool.info/thailand19/

www.DawnDelVecchio.com

http://womanspeak.com/

www.gatherthewomen.org

www.instituteforcirclework.org

https://www.wellandgood.com/good-advice/womens-circles-hosting-how-to/

http://circleconnections.com/circles/why-circles/

www.girlscouts.org/

About the author

Penelope Genter has spent a lifetime studying the face of God and how this is mirrored in all of our relationships. She outlived three husbands and has ten children and stepchildren, fifteen grandchildren, and five great-grandchildren. She is an accomplished dowser, Master Gardener, and had her own design business for over 30 years. She produced and marketed flower and gem essences, taught at university and at numerous workshops and seminars. She is a Unity of Sedona Chaplain and facilitated the Mary Magdalene Circle there for five years. She taught the 16 week *Creating Sacred Relationships Class* at Unity in early 2015 based upon Mother Mary's teachings she channeled. She facilitated a Sophia Woman's group in Sedona from 2015-2017. She now facilitates a Magdalene Mystery School in Sedona, AZ.

In 2015 Penny was one of the presenters in the Premier GODTALKS™ presentation in Sedona, AZ. This is available on YouTube and at www.godtalkssedona.com . YouTube also has her talk on **Searching for Mary Magdalene**.

Penelope has written other books with Mother Mary and her partners in spirit that are meant to inspire people to see their own inner divinity and to share this loving awareness with others on the path.

Other books by Penelope/Penny Genter

Touching Home—Roadmaps for the New Age (E-book) 1998

Returning Home—A Workbook for Ascension 2001

2013 Blueprints for the New Paradigm (E-book) 2007

Hieros Gamos – The Sacred Union of the Divine Feminine and Divine Masculine available on Amazon and Kindle.2016

Sar'h – A story of Tamar, Firstborn of Mary Magdalene and Jesus the Christ, for those with ears to hear available on Amazon, Kindle and Audible. 2017

The Messenger – Healing Breast Cancer. Following a healing path through Eastern and Western Medicine with Angelic Guidance. Available on Amazon and Kindle. 2018

Soul Weaving – Exploring the Tapestry of our Incarnations, Available on Amazon and Kindle. 2018

79

50680739R00046

Made in the USA
Columbia, SC
10 February 2019